FOREWORD

As is such in today's world, Kunchi and I found our friendship online through one of the various online BBQ platforms. I own and run alongside a team of BBQ fanatics. Whereby he furthered his BBQ education and craft, pushing himself to master the kettle, drum offset and more. Kunchi Lattore "Cookin' Wid Kunchi" has become an exceptional BBQer. While he was learning, he opened himself up to teaching and developing which has made him into a powerhouse content creator that has had a profound impact on so many people with his work, in his element of fuel, in fire management and BBQ.

As the driving force behind his beloved online community, Kunchi has single-handedly taught hundreds of thousands of people across the globe the art of elevated, flavor-packed barbecue. Through his meticulously crafted recipes, instructional videos, clips, and passionate tutorials, he has demystified techniques that were once the domain of pitmasters and comp pros. He has pulled back the veil of unnecessary effort as well as empowered home BBQers to take their grilling and smoking game to new heights. With infectious enthusiasm and a gift for making complex culinary skills accessible, Kunchi has built a loyal following who hang on to his every word, eager to learn the secrets to crafting the perfect brisket, unleashing perfect smoke penetration, that island flair, and attaining that perfection level cook that elevates barbecue from mere sustenance to a transcendent sensory experience. More than just a resource for recipes, "Cookin' Wid Kunchi" has become a community where backyard BBQers follow together to share tips, stories, & discover the joys of low-and-slow cooking.

As readers delve into Kunchi's culinary wisdom, fire management, and personal recipes contained within these pages, this foreword will serve as a warm welcome. An invitation to join the movement that is redefining what it means to master the art of Barbecue.

Wes Phillips,
The Smoke Ring Syndicate Backyard Smokers BBQ

IGNITE YOUR PASSION

The sizzle of meat, the crackle of flames, the aroma of smoke-these are the sounds and scents of backyard barbecue perfection. For many, grilling is more than just cooking; it is a passion, a gathering point for friends and family. However, those who consistently battle flare- ups or produce less-than-ideal results, the journey to barbecue bliss can feel like an uphill climb.

I've been there. The early days of my grilling adventures were filled with frustration and wasted food. I spent countless hours poring over online forums and watching endless YouTube tutorials which only made me more confused than ever. With each failed attempt, I was not just wasting food, I was gaining experience. I started seeing real improvements in my food when I began to understand the science behind fire management.

This book is my invitation to share the knowledge and experience I've gained over the years. It guides those who yearn to wrangle the fire and elevate their grilling game. Whether you are a seasoned griller looking to refine your skills, or a novice just starting, you'll find valuable insights and practical tips within these pages.

Over the years, I realized the book world was lacking in options for a comprehensive guide that demystified the art and science of barbecue. This book is my attempt to fill that void. I want to share the knowledge and experience I've gained through countless hours of grilling and experimenting. By providing practical advice and actionable tips, my hope to help you avoid my costly mistakes and achieve barbecue mastery.

Let's embark on your unique journey to barbecue bliss. It's time to wrangle the fire and unleash your grilling potential. Together, we will **explore** the distinct types of cooking equipment, cooking methods, and fuels available to you. Most importantly, we will delve into the intricacies of fire management, empowering you to create the perfect cooking environment for any occasion. With this knowledge, you'll be able to confidently tackle any barbecue challenge and produce mouthwatering results that will impress even the most discerning palate.

TABLE OF CONTENTS

1. What is fire management
2. Aspects of fire management
3. Choosing your fuel – The key to BBQ and Grilling success.
4. Maestro of airflow-Why dirty smoke is the Enemy of delicious BBQ.
5. Choose your range
6. Backyard BBQ Smackdown: Grills vs smokers
7. Kettle grills: Mastering the 22" Weber Kettle
8. Using a drum smoker
9. The backyard offset smoker
10. The Minion method
11. Summing it up
12. Recipes

WHAT IS FIRE MANAGEMENT

Fire Management for Grilling, Barbecuing, and Smoking

Many people who like the idea of grilling start with a gas grill. Many say it is easier to deal with and helps them be proficient in cooking. I promise you nobody has ever had a piece of barbeque chicken from a gas grill and says, "Man that propane just gives it that juicy zing!".

The key to achieving mouthwatering, melt-in-your-mouth grilled and smoked delicacies lies not just in your recipe or the quality of your ingredients but in your ability to harness the power and flavor of your fire. Fire management is an art form. A dance between fuel, airflow, and heat allows you to use a range of temperature control tools for a successful grill session. Mastering this key principle unlocks consistent results, turning you from backyard warrior to pitmaster (of your own pit).

Why Master the Flames?

Precise fire management ensures consistent cooking: no more dry chicken or undercooked ribs. Consistent temperatures guarantee perfectly grilled and smoked food every time. Mastering techniques like a reverse sear, where you cook low and slow and then crank heat to sear, is a game-changing skill. Fire management unlocks these powers.

Enhanced Flavor: Proper airflow prevents flare-ups and dirty smoke, which yields a distinct bitterness. This allows the true flavors of your food and smoke to marry together and satisfy the BBQ craving.

Fuel Efficiency: Understanding your fire means using less fuel, saving money, and reducing environmental impact.

ASPECTS OF FIRE MANAGEMENT

Understanding and implementing the three key factors of fire management- fuel selection, airflow and ventilation, and meat positioning- is crucial for successful grilling, barbecuing, and smoking. These aspects significantly influence the outcome of your cooking sessions, making them more successful on a regular basis. Here is a quick outline of the purpose of each. The following chapters will give a more in-depth view of each key factor.

Fuel selection

Regarding fuel selection, there is a difference between every fuel type and how they impart flavor to your proteins. For example, using just wood in an offset smoker will give you far superior flavor than if you are using a pellet smoker. It all comes down to the amount of processing this fuel type has endured.

Lump charcoal will perform better, flavor-wise, than, for example, briquets. Since lump charcoal has had limited processing, you get more of that flavor.

The only process that lump charcoal undertakes is just carbonizing from its natural wood state. So, lump charcoal is as close to burning wood as you will get when imparting flavors onto your meats.

Take from your experience of using charcoal, which is lump, wood chunks or wood chips, or pellets to cook with, and understand how those fuel types cook and the types of manipulation that you must employ to get prosperous flavor in your smoking and barbecue cooks.

The type of fuel you use also determines what type of control measures you need to employ in your cooking. You need to do more than run the minion method using straight wood as it will burn at an inconsistent pace versus using briquets to set up in a snake method. Or, if you have lump charcoal, set it up in a pile and use airflow to burn it strategically.

Let's talk about fuel:

Charcoal is the classic choice for grilling and barbecuing. Opt for high quality charcoal with consistent hardwood lumps or briquets made from lump charcoal with zero chemical additives. *Lump charcoal* is superior due to its consistent heat and clean-burning nature. *Briquettes*, the high-quality ones, burn evenly and at a slower pace due to their dense and compact design.

Wood is the king of smoking, infusing food with unique aromas. Different woods use their naturally occurring oils to impart immense flavors that pair with the subsequent smoke. Choose hardwoods like *oak, hickory,* or *mesquite* for slow cooking, and fruitwoods like *cherry* or *apple* for lighter fare.

Gas is clean, convenient, and precise; gas grills offer instant heat control. Use a quality gas grill with multiple burners for optimal heat distribution.

Airflow and ventilation

Airflow and ventilation play a significant role in the cooking process. Without oxygen, there is no fire. With too much oxygen, there is too much fire. Being able to manipulate your fire and your grill into a situation where the airflow is exactly right is a key aspect of fire management. This skill allows you to hold a successful grill session that is comfortable and will give you the results that you are looking for.

Understanding how to position your intake versus your exhaust is crucial when it comes to smoking barbecue, using a smoker, or even using a grill. These are the factors that determine how successful your cooking session is going to be. Mastering these skills will make you feel in control and confident in your cooking.

Airflow: The Maestro of the Flame

No matter, if you are grilling, barbecuing, or smoking, knowing how to position your dampers or vents, will help you control the amount of oxygen reaching the fire, influencing its intensity and smoke level. Open dampers allow for a hotter fire while closed dampers allow the fire to be at a lower heat.

The latter yields more smoke flavor. This occurs as the meat is cooking slowly and will be in there much longer allowing plenty of time for the smoke flavor from the wood to penetrate the meat.

Some grill vents can be manipulated to allow a grill to operate as a smoker when it wasn't the intended design. This practice can affect direct and indirect heat zones when you are working with a singular cooking chamber but want to attain that low and slow precision.

Meat Positioning: Where you put your meat matters.

Fire management techniques reach far beyond that just the type of smoker you have or the fuel you use. Be deliberate and specific where you are placing your meat on your smoker so that your meat can successfully take on the flavors you are trying to impart. For the best results you need to have the meat between the intake and the exhaust somewhere between the fire.

Using some of the straightforward grill set ups I will be reviewing in this book will help you understand how to position your meat on the smoker in relation to the intake and exhaust to create some amazing, family gathering worthy B-B-Q sessions!

Using indirect setups with wood and charcoal has significant benefits for you as a backyard enthusiast. You can close your lid and walk away for a bathroom break, check on the kids or even grab a cold beer. All the while, your food will continue to cook slowly and not get charred to oblivion. When you are back to the smoker, then you can bring the meat to the direct heat and finish the cook and be in control of your sear and or crisp. Clean smoke imparts delicious flavor, and the direct heat gives you the look you want.

Universal Truths:

These principles apply to all grill types, from charcoal barrels to fancy gas rigs. With practice and some fireside wisdom, you'll be a grilling and smoking pro in no time. Remember, fire is a powerful tool. Respect it and understand it, and it will reward you with culinary masterpieces.

So remember, the next time you light up the grill or smoker, know that you are the conductor of the flame orchestra. By mastering fire management, you'll compose a symphony of smoky flavors and juicy perfection.

CHOOSING YOUR FUEL
THE **KEY TO BBQ AND GRILLING** SUCCESS

The right fuel can elevate your barbecue and grill from ordinary to extraordinary. Each fuel type imparts unique flavors and heating properties, so understanding their strengths is critical to selecting the best one for your culinary creations.

WOOD

Wood chunks and splits are the gold standard for smoky flavor. Hickory adds a robust and savory taste with a hint of sweetness. Most oak varieties provide a milder smoke that complements many foods, while post oak kisses sweetness. Fruitier woods like apple and cherry impart a mild smoke flavor, but the color of cherry is king. Understanding the different flavors will allow you to make a more informed decision when choosing what wood to pair with what protein or dish you smoke.

LUMP CHARCOAL

Lump charcoal is pure carbonized hardwood, unlike briquets, which are compressed pieces with other ingredients. This means lump charcoal burns hotter and cleaner while imparting a richer, more natural flavor to your food.

Here's why lump charcoal is the grilling champion: Lump charcoal is known for its highlights and heat reach, which allows it to reach sear temperatures more quickly than most other fuels. This makes it perfect for steaks and juicy burgers.

This is one of the cleaner-burning fuels for grilling, smoking, and barbecuing. Less ash and smoke mean less bitterness and more delicious flavor. Producing less ash means less waste and less maintenance for your firebox.

The natural wood flavor of lump charcoal enhances the taste of your food for a true grilling experience. Since lump charcoal is made from partially burnt wood, it still retains some of the wood's natural oils to impart those bold flavors we desire.

BRIQUETS

Charcoal briquets, uniform black squares, are the unsung heroes of countless backyard barbecues. Beneath their unassuming exterior lies a surprising amount of science and design. Let's delve into the briquets world, exploring how they're made and the thought behind their shapes.

The process begins with charcoal dust, a byproduct of burning wood, typically used to make lump charcoal. This dust is mixed with a binder, often a natural material like starch or clay. Water is added to create a moldable paste, which is then pressed into shapes using specialized machinery. The formed briquets are then dried, a crucial step that ensures they burn efficiently.

The design of briquets goes beyond mere aesthetics. The uniform shape allows for optimal grill packing and promotes even airflow. This results in consistent heat distribution. The compact form also help maximize the amount of fuel within a limited space.

While some briquets are purely composed of charcoal and natural binders, others may include additives like lighter fluid or other chemicals to enhance the burn time. These additives can shorten grilling prep time but beware it may impart a slight chemical flavor to your food. Opting for natural briquets ensures a pure flavor profile.

Some companies have taken the briquets further and made charlogs (charcoal logs). These are made from the same materials as the briquets but are shaped like logs with a hole extruded through the center. The density and shape give these charlogs a superpower. They have a slower burn rate, and when they are all lit, they are scorching hot. They are suited for low, slow, and open- fire cooking as they can be a good long-burning base for wood splits or chunks.

Competition Oak Briquets

Texas Style B&B Competition Oak Briquets are a favorite among champion pitmasters because of their long and clean burn. Competition charcoal briquets create an optimal amount of smoke, burning at low or high temperatures, which produces that great smoky flavor you're looking for.

- Briquets made from oak
- No chemical additives or fillers
- Burns hotter, longer, cleaner
- Available in 8.8 and 17.6 lb. bags

Where to buy?

MAESTRO OF AIRFLOW

Why dirty smoke is the enemy of delicious BBQ

Imagine tending to your smoker for hours, only to end up with a bitter, acrid-tasting barbecue. The culprit? Dirty smoke. Unlike the thin, wispy smoke that imparts a pleasant flavor, dirty smoke arises from incomplete combustion, infusing your food with unwanted chemicals. This method causes terrible taste, but your meat will appear black and not be a "bark." The easiest way to identify if your meat was prepared with dirty smoke is to swipe your finger across the surface. If a black, greasy substance appears like tar, that meat is cooked with dirty smoke.

Dirty smoke, when it touches the tongue, causes a numbing bitterness. Other indicators include strong smoke in your refrigerator for multiple days if you store leftovers, indigestion, which causes you to belch the acrid smoke flavor for days because the body cannot process it, and black stains over your cutting boards and containers, which are also a telltale sign that you are cooking with dirty smoke.

Scientifically, dirty smoke forms when insufficient oxygen restricts the fuel source's ability to burn consistently. This lack of oxygen produces large, unburnt molecules that coat your meat with a sooty residue. These unburnt molecules are unpleasant to taste and harmful if consumed in large quantities.

Another factor is wet wood. The practice of cooking with damp wood is still prevalent today. Certain brands even promote it by encouraging consumers to soak wood chips and chunks to get "more smoke." You will see more smoke, but it doesn't necessarily translate into deliciousness. NO WET WOOD. EVER

The actual flavor of your food lies mainly in the oils emitted from burning a particular wood or fuel. The smoke, coincidentally, is merely a byproduct of the process of burning wood. When used appropriately, it should be used as a complimentary part of the flavor profile, which is comprised of the meat, your seasonings, the oils from the wood, and a proportionate amount of clean smoke. Dirty smoke will overwhelm your profile, compromising your outcome with too much of one thing. Once you have tasted the difference between dirty and clean smoke, you will never want dirty smoked food again.

To accomplish clean smoke that yields the best flavor, you first need to identify the path or direction of the airflow. It would help if you located the intake and the exhaust on your smoker. Fire placement must always be close to the intake so that the airflow drags the heat and smoke from the heat towards the exhaust where the meat should be. If you run a small fire or a small amount of lit charcoal, you can open your intake as wide as possible to carry the maximum heat towards the meat. Inversely, if you have more coals lit, then restrict the opening at the intake, and then if you still need more control, make minor adjustments to the exhaust as well. This principle is applied throughout my methods in this book, everywhere from the snake and minion methods to running the offset. Refer to those specific chapters.

Identifying dirty smoke is relatively easy. It's thick, white or black, and billows out of your smoker in large plumes. Clean smoke, on the other hand, is thin and

usually has a bluish hue. The misconception that more smoke equals better BBQ is a persistent one. In reality, an abundance of dirty smoke overwhelms your food with harsh flavors.

The ideal scenario is to achieve a thin layer of clean smoke that gently infuses your barbecue with a smoky taste.

So, how do you avoid dirty smoke? Always practice good fire management. Adjust your smoker's vents to ensure proper airflow. The delicate balance of airflow and heat, along with the appropriate fuel, creates the delicious heat and smoke we crave on our smoked meats. Use dry, seasoned wood and avoid mistakes like overloading the firebox, using wet wood, or choking out your fire. By achieving clean combustion, you'll be well on your way to perfectly smoked barbecue.

WRANGLING FIRE Achunchigan Lattore

WRANGLING FIRE Achunchigan Lattore

CHOOSE YOUR RANGE

Two types of heat:

Direct heat: Ideal for searing steaks or grilling burgers. Place food directly over the hottest coals.

Indirect heat: perfect for slow-cooking roasts or pulled pork. Position food away from the heat source and use the reflected heat for gentle cooking.

Fire Size Matters

Grilling: Start with a medium-hot fire for searing and high-heat cooking, gradually tapering to medium for slower grilling. Burgers, steaks, boneless chicken and pork chops are typically done this way.

Barbecuing: For long cooking times, maintain a low and slow fire. Build a base of hot coals and replenish with smaller pieces of wood or charcoal as needed. Barbecuing is very versatile and can be used to cook many meats such as ribs, larger steaks and small roasts, chicken with the bone in and skin on.

Smoking: Aim for a steady, low temperature (around 200-250°F) for even smoke penetration. Use smaller wood chunks or splits to maintain consistent heat. This method is perfect for larger and typically tougher cuts that will take a longer time to breakdown. Pork butts, large roasts, briskets and even ribs are the ideal meats for this temp range.

BACKYARD BBQ SMACKDOWN
Grills Vs Smokers

You can choose just one, or you can have 'em all.

The Rundown:

The backyard grill is a summertime staple, but the grilling world extends far beyond burgers and hotdogs. For the discerning pitmaster, a whole universe of smokers offers unique cooking styles and results. Let's dive into five popular options to help you pick your perfect cooker.

The Weber Kettle Grill: This American classic is a favorite for its versatility and affordability. Using charcoal briquets, the kettle provides direct heat for searing steaks or indirect heat for slow roasting. While not a dedicated smoker, it can achieve smoky results using wood chips and a water pan.

Kamado Grills: These Japanese-inspired ceramic cookers are known for their exceptional heat retention and efficiency. They excel at low-and-slow smoking but can also sear at extremely high temperatures. Kamados require lump charcoal and are known for producing consistent smoke flavor.

Offset Smokers: These traditional smokers feature a firebox connected to a separate smoke chamber. By controlling the firebox temperature, you can achieve low and slow smoking for perfectly tender, juicy meats. Offset smokers require practice to manage the fire but offer a deep, wood-fired flavor.

Drum Smokers: These budget-friendly smokers are often converted from recycled oil drums. They use charcoal and wood chips for smoking, offering reasonable temperature control and a decent cooking space. Drum smokers may leak some smoke and require more frequent fuel management.

Center Flow Smokers: These vertical smokers use a central charcoal basket to distribute heat evenly. They're known for their ease of use and ability to maintain consistent temperatures, making them ideal for beginners. Center-flow smokers may not impart as much smoky flavor as other options, unless you know how to manage your heat and airflow to slow down the cook process.

The best smoker or grill depends on your priorities. An offset smoker or kamado grill might be ideal if you crave smoky, competition-worthy BBQ. A Weber kettle or center- flow smoker could be perfect for beginners or those seeking versatility. Drum smokers offer a budget-friendly option for casual smoking enthusiasts. No matter your choice, with some practice, you'll be a backyard BBQ champion in no time.

Here's a quick comparison to help you decide:

Feature	Weber Kettle	Kamado Grill	Offset Smoker	Drum Smoker	Center Flow Grill/Smoker
Cooking Style	Grilling, Smoking (Excellent)	Grilling, Smoking (Excellent)	Smoking (Excellent)	Smoking {Good}	Smoking (Easy)
Fuel	Charcoal Briquets	Lump Charcoal	Charcoal	Charcoal	Charcoal or Electric
Temp Control	Moderate	Excellent	Challenging	Moderate	Easy
Smoke Flavor	Mild	Excellent	Deep, Wood-Fired	Moderate	Mild
Versatility	High	High	Moderate	Moderate	Low
Price	Low	High	Moderate	Low	Low
Ease of Use	Easy	Moderate	Challenging	Easy	Easy
Ideal Method(s)	Snake method, Indirect, Direct grilling.	Minion method Direct grilling	Run with a small fire, use airflow to control temps.	Minion Method for low heat or high heat cooking	Minion method, Direct grilling

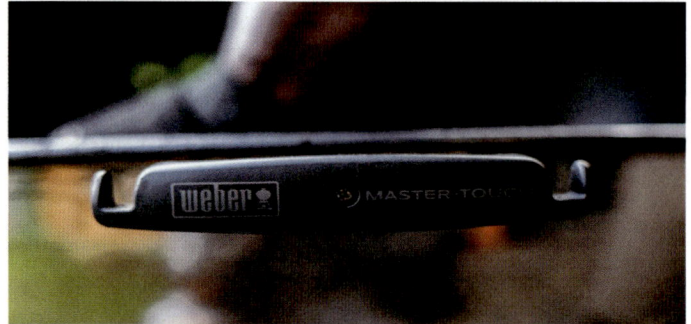

KETTLE GRILLS

With their simple design and functionality, Kettle grills have been a backyard staple for decades. But be aware of their unassuming look; these grills are surprisingly versatile for smoking, grilling, and barbecuing.

A Brief History of Kettle Grills:

The Weber Kettle, invented in 1952, is widely considered the original kettle grill. It transformed backyard grilling with its closed-lid design, which allowed for indirect heat and controlled airflow, perfect for low and slow cooking.

Versatility at Its Finest:

Today's charcoal kettle grills offer even more versatility. New charcoal products like lump charcoal and briquets allow you to tailor your cooking method to achieve different results.

Smoking with the Snake Method:

For low and slow smoking, the snake method is a popular choice. By arranging charcoal briquets in a specific pattern around the edge of the grill, you can create a long, slow burn that's perfect for smoking meats like brisket and pork butt.

Beyond Smoking

Of course, kettle grills excel at high-heat grilling, too. Sear steaks, burgers, and vegetables to juicy perfection. And don't forget barbecuing - kettle grills can easily handle slow-cooking ribs or chicken with smoky flavor.

So next time you fire up your kettle grill, remember it's not a one-trick pony. With a bit of creativity and the proper techniques, you can use it to create a wide variety of delicious grilled and smoked foods.

Mastering The Weber Kettle Using The Snake Method

The snake method is a long-proven technique for low and slow cooking on your Weber Kettle. It's perfect for smoking briskets, pork shoulders, ribs, and other delicious cuts that require extended cooking times.

Here's how to set it up:

1. **Gather your supplies:**

- Unlit charcoal briquets (B&B briquets recommended)
- Wood chunks for smoke
- Charcoal chimney and fire starter

2. **Form the snake:**

- Arrange your unlit briquets around the outer edge of the grill, standing them on their ends in a domino-like fashion. Each briquet should touch the next, ensuring a continuous burn.
- Leave a small gap between the two ends for lighting.
- If using a drip pan, place it in the middle of the snake.

3. **Light the snake:**

- Light 6-8 briquets in your chimney.
- When they ash over, place the briquets at one end of the charcoal setup.
- Allow 45 minutes for the grill to heat up, clean your grates, and add a drip pan.

4. **Adjust the vents:**

- Open both vents fully to allow for good air circulation.
- If your temperature rises above 225-250 degrees start

by adjusting the bottom vents. Also, note that the snake can take up to 2 hours to reach its plateau temperature, so don't be in a rush. Add meat after 185° or more.
- Ensure that the top vents are opposite the hot end of your snake to draw smoke and heat across your meat.

Tips for success:

- Use good quality charcoal like B&B Competition Oak briquets or something comparable.
- Ensure your briquets touch the grill surface to remain primed and reduce dirty smoke.
- This is no need to monitor the temperature regularly. Adjust the vents only if needed.

Benefits of the snake method:

- Long cooks: The snake method can provide up to 16 hours of cooking time without adding additional fuel.
- Consistent temperature: The gradual burning of the briquets helps maintain a stable and consistent cooking temperature.
- Fuel efficiency: You'll only need two layers of briquets for extended cooking, making it fuel-efficient.
- Great flavor: The indirect heat generated by the snake method produces smoky and flavorful results.

With some practice, you'll be a pro at using the snake method to create delicious and tender smoked meats on your Weber Kettle!

USING A DRUM SMOKER

Mastering Your Drum Smoker

The drum smoker, a DIV favorite or a store-bought powerhouse, offers incredible versatility at an attractive price point. However, its large capacity and simple design can be intimidating for beginners. This guide will unveil the secrets of running your drum smoker and explore the worlds of hot and fast cooks alongside the low and slow barbecue classics.

First things first, fire it up! Most drum smokers utilize a charcoal basket for heat. Fill it with lump charcoal, briquets, or even charlogs. Light it with a fire starter, and once glowing red coals have formed in place of your starter, give it some time to get the appropriate fire size. I can't tell you how long it takes to open, but here is what I do: keep it open for another 10-15 minutes and then close the lid. Open both vents wide open and see where your temperature falls. If you are below 175 degrees, try opening for another 5 minutes and repeat the process.

Once you get to within 50 degrees of your target temperature, start to close down your intake and allow that smoke to run clean. Then, you are ready to add wood chunks, your heat deflector, and your meat. Vents are critical for temperature control. If you use an analog thermometer, give it about 1.5-2 hrs to let the temperature get right. Once your smoke is running clean, add your meat and walk away. When you return, your temperature should be close to, or exactly where you want it.

Here's My Hum on the Drum:

Low and Slow: This is where drum smokers shine. Target temperatures between 225-275°F (107-135°C) are ideal for long cooks like brisket, pork shoulder, or ribs. The thick steel walls retain heat remarkably well, allowing for consistent smoking for hours.

Hot and Fast: Consider the drum smoker's ability to crank the heat! By lighting more fuel in the charcoal basket and opening the vents fully, you can achieve temperatures exceeding 350°F (177°C). It is perfect for techniques like reverse searing steaks, aiming for crispy skin on poultry, or grilling burgers, all while infusing them with a beautiful smoky flavor.

Smoke Signals: Wood Selection

Wood chunks are your ticket to smoky paradise. Different woods impart unique flavors, so experiment to find your favorites. Hickory is a classic for ribs and pork, while fruit woods like apple or cherry add a touch of sweetness to chicken or fish.

For low and slow cooks, add a handful of wood chunks directly to the coals when you get the fire lit. This method creates a burst of smoke early on and tapers off as the coals burn down, leaving a subtle smokiness throughout the cook.

For hot and fast cooks, there will be somewhat less smoke flavor, but it will still be delicious. Add wood chunks as you usually would and enjoy the subtle smokey goodness.

Beyond Barbecue: Unveiling Versatility

The drum smoker's prowess extends far beyond just barbecue. Here are some unexpected ways to utilize your smoker:

Pizza Perfection: For pizzeria-worthy results, use a pizza stone preheated in the smoker. The high heat creates a crispy crust with a hint of smoke, elevating your homemade pizzas.

Smoking Cheese: Experiment with smoking various cheeses for a unique appetizer or cheeseboard addition. Try gouda for a deep, nutty flavor or cheddar for a hint of smokiness.

Smoking Vegetables: Don't relegate vegetables to the side dish category! Smoked vegetables like eggplant, peppers, or onions take on a depth of flavor that compliments any main course. The drum smoker's vast temperature range allows you to grill, smoke, and barbecue always.

A Smoky Rival: Drum Smoker vs. Offset Smoker

The Drum Smoker can be compared to the Offset Smoker, which is the king of low and slow cooking. While offset smokers offer a more traditional design, drum smokers hold their own. Their thick steel construction retains heat exceptionally well, rivaling the performance of offset smokers at a fraction of the cost. The ability to achieve high heat for hot and fast cooks adds another dimension of versatility to the drum smoker's repertoire. The drum smoker performs very differently with different types of fuels. For example, a basket of lump charcoal running 225- 250 in my drum can last me between 12-14 hours without needing to reload. I can get 18-20 hours for briquets at those same temperatures. The charlogs reign supreme with 34 hours continuously on one single load. With some practice, you'll be a drum smoker master, churning out everything from melt-in-your-mouth barbecue to smoky pizzas. So, grab your favorite cut of meat, some wood chunks, and your favorite charcoal, and get ready to unlock the full potential of your drum smoker!

COMPETITION CHAR-LOGS

- Expert's choice for real wood smoke flavor
- Made from real hardwood and vegetable starch
- No chemical additives or fillers
- Burns hotter, longer, cleaner
- Available in 15 and 30 lb. bags

Derived from hardwood, these unique, hollow, log-shaped briquets are a favorite among world champion pitmasters because of their long, clean burn. But don't worry, you don't need to be an expert to use these versatile char logs. Their shape aids them in controlling the taste profile while delivering winning flavor. Fire up B&B Char-Logs in charcoal grills such as kettles, ceramic grills, and more, as well as smokers and pizza ovens. The mild flavor from these Texas-style Competition Char Logs works great with any meat or side.

The Backyard Offset

The BBQ Nemesis or THE BEST THING EVER

True offset mastery is desired by almost all BBQ enthusiasts, and for good reason. The best flavor in BBQ will always live in offset cooking. Now, don't be fooled, this machine requires a great understanding of airflow relative to the size of your fire. In this publication, and in all my related video content, I show you how to master this very concept of fire management.

Fire management in BBQ cooking, whether on a dedicated smoker or on a grill being used as a smoker, hinges on a few basic principles. The airflow must be sufficient to bring heat and smoke from the fire. Conversely, the heat must match your desired temperature. Many of us struggle with fire management for the simple fact that the fire is too big.

Due to my understanding of the dynamics of heat versus airflow, I always opt to start the smallest fire possible, especially when smoking. Grilling is different, since you need higher heat, but in this situation I employ a two-zone configuration more often than not. With barbecuing, I use less heat than grilling, but I typically use distance to ensure my meat cooks evenly without burning. I consider these a few cardinal fireside principles that I employ, all the time.

Specifically, with the offsets, a small fire, proper heat diffusion, and proper airflow from intake to exhaust are the most important relationships to understand. If you are interested in getting into offset cooking, I urge you to understand these principles. Practice them until you have a good handle on it. The offset will always be the monster that it is, so do not expect it to get easier. The process of adding splits when necessary, checking on fire vitality to prevent dirty smoke, and even managing split sizes are all linchpins of what makes the offset the king of the patio. Instead, with your repetition of the process, the process will become more of a custom.

Offset cooking is a ritualistic dance, which, once mastered, becomes a graceful flow. Efficiently running your offset smoker in a specific temperature range and achieving clean smoke will yield consistent results that encompass beautiful bark on your meats and an unmistakable smoke flavor.

Step by Step: How To Fire Up A Backyard Offset Smoker

1. Fire up ½ chimneys of lump charcoal or briquets. I prefer lump charcoal because it produces less ash.

2. Select appropriate size (dry/seasoned) wood splits for your smoker. I prefer 10-12 inches, around the thickness of my forearm. It won't be exact.

3. Clean out the firebox to remove ash from the previous cook. This helps to maximize airflow throughout the cook.

4. When the charcoal is lit, start building your fire. I typically start with 1-2 logs on top of my bed of charcoal.

5. Try to keep the charcoal to one side of the basket. This method lets you build a more concentrated fire that will burn better and keep your fire more robust for longer.

6. While my smoker is heating up, I like to place my splits inside to get primed (more ready for combustion).

7. Give your fire about 20-30 minutes to get your smoker up to optimal temperature. If you need more heat, add a small split. When the smoke from the stack is translucent and not foul-smelling, you are ready to cook.

8. Run a small fire. This way, you can have optimal control over your temperatures. To make a small fire effective, give it a lot of airflow from the intake. Also, open your exhaust so it drags that heat through the smoker.

9. A baffle plate inside your smoker is important for distributing heat from left to right. Scour the internet for the one that best fits your model.

10. Your temperature should run in a particular range that you choose. The size of your fire will determine if you stay between 225-250 when your temperature starts to drop below 230°, that's when you add another split or two. Based on the size, density and dryness of your wood splits, this should keep your fire where you desire for another 30 minutes to an hour.

In my offset cooking operation, I have certain things that remain true among all my backyard pits. The splits will last me between 30-45 minutes, if I am running between 225-250. My heat will be more evenly distributed across the cook chamber when there is a heat deflector or baffle plate in use. The higher the temperature runs in the offset, the less efficient the temperatures will run over time. Your airflow is one of the most important factors that guide your cooks in the offset.

WRANGLING FIRE Achunchigan Lattore

The Minion Method
Turn your drum smoker & kamado into a charcoal sipper

My Opinion on the Minion:

The Essence of Low and Slow:
Low and slow cooking is a deliberate dance between time and temperature. We're talking about hours spent in the 225-250°F (110-120°C) range, patiently coaxing collagen to melt and flavors to deepen. This magic transform tough cuts like pulled pork shoulders and beef briskets into melt-in-your-mouth masterpieces.

When is the Minion Method Appropriate?
The minion method is truly versatile, but it should be reserved for specific units to maximize fuel efficiency and performance. This method will transform your drum, bullet, center flow, kettles, and kamado-style smokers into legit smoking machines with the coveted "set it and forget it" precision and control.

Why the Minion Method Reigns Supreme
The Minion Method is your key to unlocking low and slow heaven. It revolves around setting up the charcoal, ensuring long-lasting, even heat without constant refueling. Here's how it works:

1. **Charcoal Symphony or Chaos:**
   Start by loading your charcoal basket with lump charcoal, briquets, or charcoal logs. You can either dump them in or stack and layer them neatly.

2. **Ignite the Spark:**
   Now, light a fire starter either on the edge for low and slow cooking or in the center for medium-high heat cooking. You can use a chimney starter and then dump coals into one spot, but the fire starter is more precise. These lit coals will act as the engine, gradually igniting the surrounding charcoal pieces as they burn down. All you have to do is control the

amount of oxygen going through the intake, and you are on course.

3. Patience is Key:
Resist the urge to fiddle! Let the lit coals work their magic, slowly creeping outward and lighting the unlit charcoal. It can take 30-45 minutes to reach your desired range but trust the process.

4. Smoke Signals:
Once the temperature is within range, add your dry-smoking wood chunks or chips (optional but highly recommended for extra smoky goodness). Now, place your food on the grate, adjust the airflow vents for desired temperature control, and settle in for the slow- cooking saga.

5. Charcoal Matters: Fueling Flavor, Not Chemicals
The Minion Method isn't just about convenience; it's about purity. Using high-quality natural charcoal ensures your food is kissed by smoke, not unwanted chemical nasties. Here's why good charcoal matters:
Natural Ingredients: For the cleanest burn and best flavor, opt for charcoal made from hardwood or lump charcoal. Avoid charcoal with chemical additives and fillers.
Consistent Heat: Quality charcoal burns longer and more evenly, maintaining that essential low and slow temperature for hours.
Pure Smoke: Chemical-free charcoal produces clean smoke that enhances your food's flavor without any off- putting tastes or residues.

6. Minion Method Magic
The Minion Method offers a plethora of benefits for your low and slow BBQ adventures:
Set it and forget it: Enjoy extended cooking times without worrying about adding charcoal. Relax, sip a

beer, and let the smoker do its thing.

Consistent Temperature: Say goodbye to temperature fluctuations. The Minion Method maintains a steady heat, ensuring perfectly cooked results.

Clean Smoke Flavor: Ditch the chemical-tinged smoke. Good charcoal delivers pure, woodsy smoke that infuses your food with authentic BBQ goodness.

7. **Mastering the Minion Method**

   With some practice, the Minion Method will become your go-to technique for low and slow BBQ glory. Here are some additional tips for success:

- Use the appropriate amount of fuel.
- Use the proper amount of charcoal for your smoker size.
- Start with slightly less lit charcoal than you might need, as excess charcoal can create unwanted heat.
- Remember, it is easy to increase heat, but trying to calm it down can be hell.

   Wood Chucking Wisdom: Introduce smoking wood chunks or chips early in the process for maximum smoke infusion. Dry-seasoned wood is best for the purest of smoke flavors. Wet wood will produce more smoke but terrible flavor.

   Independent Thermometer: This will be your trusty guide. Based on placement and other factors, most stock thermometers on smokers are not 100% accurate. Refrain from relying on guesswork. Invest in a good digital thermometer to monitor your fire's performance independently.

The Final Sizzle

The Minion Method is more than just a charcoal arrangement; it's a gateway to BBQ nirvana. The enjoyment of cooking will be immense, especially when you don't have to fight with fire to get the best results. So, fire up your smoker, embrace the low and slow philosophy, and let the Minion Method guide you to melt- in-your-mouth BBQ masterpieces. Remember, good food and quality ingredients take time and patience. With the Minion Method as your trusty sidekick, you'll be a BBQ specialist in no time! Happy smoking!

B&B Charcoal

The #1 Recommended charcoal brand from KUNCHI

"With B&B Charcoal I don't need to sacrifice flavor for performance."
KUNCHI

WRANGLING FIRE Achunchigan Lattore

SUMMING *it* UP

The Flame Within

As I conclude this journey into the world of fire management, I hope you now feel equipped and inspired to transform your backyard into a culinary haven. Wrangling fire is a skill that develops over time, requiring patience, practice, and a healthy dose of experimentation. But remember, every barbecue is a unique adventure, and the joy lies not just in the final product, but in the process itself. The sizzle of the grill, the aroma of the smoke, and the anticipation of the first bite are the moments that make grilling a truly exhilarating experience.

I've shared my knowledge and experiences with you, hoping that it will ignite your passion for grilling. Your success is my ultimate reward. Be ready to fire up your favorite smoker and begin your culinary exploration.

The journey doesn't end here. I have included some of my favorite recipes, many of which were born from the lessons learned throughout this book. From succulent steaks to smoky brisket and everything in between, these recipes are a testament to the power of excellent fire management. I hope they inspire you to create your signature dishes.

Thank you for joining me on this barbecue adventure. Your enthusiasm, your questions, and your shared experiences have made this journey truly special. May your grills always be hot and your food always delicious.

WRANGLING FIRE Achunchigan Lattore

My Ten Favorite RECIPES

by Cookin' Wild Ranch

ACHUNCHIGAN LATTORE

"There's always room at my table, but in case you can't make it to my table, this is how you can Cook Wid Kunchi" Kunchi

NOT A CHEF

When I am by the fire, a certain feeling takes over. You can call it joy, enthusiasm, or even love. I call it passion. This passion has been the driving force that has led me to create this work- giving you an in depth look into my kitchen. But it's also been the secret ingredient in my results, daily. Wrangling Fire is more than just a guide to fire management; it's a culinary journey where the flames dictate the flavor. The power is yours, over the fire of course.

From Kunchi, with smoke.

JAMAICAN JERK CHICKEN

Runchin' Favorite

INGREDIENTS

Jamaican Jerk wet marinade
Dry Jerk seasoning
Chicken halves

STEPS

Separate chicken into halves. This recipe will also work with any cut of chicken.

Use finger to get between skin and meat to rub wet marinade there.

Season the skin side and the meat side with the dry jerk seasoning.

Allow to marinate for a few hrs. Overnight for best results.

Cook chicken in your desired smoker between 300-350° F until breast meat is cooked.

Season with love

Fire Treatment

AUTHENTIC *Jamaican* JERK MARINADE

INGREDIENTS

1 large yellow onion
1 bunch green onions
2 bulb garlic
1 thumb of ginger
1 bunch fresh thyme
2 tbsp white vinegar
2 tbsp vegetable oil
1 fresh orange squeezed or ¼ cup OJ
Add ¼ orange peel from fresh orange
2 tbsp of browning or molasses for color
5 tbsp dry jerk seasoning
5 Scotch Bonnet peppers. 2 green, 3 ripe. Leave green ones whole and remove seeds from ripened peppers for a mild marinade. Leave all seeds and membranes in for more spice. Add more salt if you want it more salty.

STEPS

Blend all the ingredients in a food processor or a blender. If you want it less liquid then reduce oil and vinegar amounts. Use it to marinate your meat overnight. Store in the refrigerator for up to 12 months.

WRANGLING FIRE Achunchigan Lattore

DRY JAMAICAN JERK RUB

INGREDIENTS

5 tbsp kosher salt
3 tbsp granulated garlic
3 tbsp granulated onion
2 tbsp red pepper flakes
2 tsp ground allspice
2 tsp ground ginger
1 tsp coriander
1 tsp ground thyme
½ tbsp dried thyme
½ tbsp ground cinnamon
1 tbsp chili powder
1 tbsp crushed whole allspice
1 tbsp whole allspice
½ tsp nutmeg

STEPS

Mix these together to get your Jamaican jerk dry rub.

JAMAICAN JERK RIBS

INGREDIENTS

Spare ribs or baby backs
Jamaican Jerk Rub

STEPS

In your smoker, running between 250-275°, place your ribs indirectly and allow to smoke for two whole hrs before you even look at it. If you'd like to wrap, wrap after the three hr mark, when the bark looks good to you. Butcher paper will give you a more solid bark but still moist, foil will allow your meat to steam more and potentially sweat the bark off. No wrap ribs are awesome, and that's my preferred way these days. With foil, more moisture is possible if you don't overcook the ribs. Total cook time for Spare ribs should be about 3½-4 hrs using this method. Give or take depending on the thickness of your ribs.

No spritz, no binder needed. And for the love of BBQ, NO WET WOOD.

HOW TO TURN SPARE RIBS INTO ST. LOUIS CUT RIBS

STEPS

Identify the fat seam that dictates the rib joint

Cut along that fat seem to separate the rib tips (rib joint) from the spare ribs.

Now you have St. Louis cut/style ribs (trimmed spare ribs).

Entire rib tip comes off.

SMOKED SKILLET CORNBREAD

INGREDIENTS

2 box jiffy honey cornbread
1 can cream corn
1 can sweet corn drained
1 stick softened butter
1 additional stick of butter
¼ cup of milk
2 eggs

STEPS

In a 12 inch skillet, melt ½ stick of butter while the grill is preheating. Mix in a bowl corn, cornbread mix, 1 stick melted butter, eggs and ½ your milk mixture. Mix until well combined. Add more milk if needed. Should be a thick batter consistency. Pour batter in the hot skillet and bake at 350° in the smoker until a toothpick comes out clean. Around 45-55 mins. When finished, melt the remaining ½ stick of butter and glaze the top of the cornbread and the edges.

GRILLED PEACH COBBLER

INGREDIENTS
6 ripened peaches
(Peeled and quartered)
1 cup brown sugar
8 tbsp butter or shortening

Batter
1 cup flour
1 cup sugar
2 tsp baking powder
¼ tsp salt
1 can evaporated milk

STEPS

Over hot coals, grill up Peeled and quartered peaches. Just grill marks and light charring. Slice peaches and put in a cast iron pan over the fire with brown sugar. Cook over high heat until the peaches are slightly soft and the sugar makes a rich syrup. Mix all batter ingredients together in a separate bowl. In a 12 inch cast iron skillet, melt butter. Remove from the smoker and pour batter into the hot skillet. Use a spoon or spatula to spread the Batter around. Spoon peaches and syrup into the batter as evenly as possible. Top with ground cinnamon. Cook in a smoker around 350-375°F for 40 minutes. Remove from the smoker and serve warm. Topped with whipped cream or vanilla ice cream.

Reverse Seared Steaks

Ingredients

Steaks
SPOG Rub
Chimichurri

Steps

In your smoker running around 250-275°F, place room temp steaks indirect of heat. When steaks get to your desired temperature, remove from heat, allow charcoal to get hot and Sear steaks until the appropriate doneness. For medium rare, stop cooking around 115°F and then sear until 125°F

Chimichurri Compound Butter

2 sticks Butter
4 cloves garlic(or more)
1 small bunch cilantro
½ shallot
1 tsp red pepper flakes
Red wine vinegar
1 tbsp olive oil
Sea salt
1 lime

Directions
Allow your Butter to get to room temperature. Use the sea salt to chop, then crush the garlic into a paste so its a better consistency for the Butter. The juice from one lime and a splash of red wine vinegar will add that acidity of a Chimichurri, as well as a splash of a rich robust olive oil. Combine all the ingredients and roll into a log inside a piece of saran wrap. Place in refrigerator for at least 30 mins to solidify for better handling. After your steak has finished cooking, add pads of butter, within reason and rest for 20 minutes. Slice and enjoy.

Fresh Chimichurri

Ingredients
1 bunch Cilantro
4-6 cloves garlic
1 fresh red chili pepper
½ shallots
2 tbsp Red Wine Vinegar
½ cup olive oil
1 tbsp Coarse sea salt
½ lime

Directions
Finely chop 1 bunch of Cilantro leaves, the shallot and garlic cloves. Place all dry ingredients in a bowl. Start by adding ½ of your olive oil until you get the consistency you want. You may end up using more than a ½ cup. Add the splash of Red Wine Vinegar to round out the flavors as well as ½ of a lime.

Snake method brisket for the win....

This is how I do it to get these killer results.

Dry brine
Dry brine with your rub or just salt overnight. My favorite salt is kosher salt for a dry brine or a rub with kosher salt. This rub in the video was my homemade SPOG blend. (1:2:1:1). When seasoning, no binder is needed. The dry rub overnight will create a dry exterior, which gives you a better bark.

Trim or not?
Doesn't matter. If you are comfortable with a knife, trim, if not, let it ride. Trimming is purely for aesthetics.

Fat cap up or down?
I cook the fat cap down. Doesn't matter how you do it. I like how my bark comes out this way. What I do focus on is placing the flat between the head and tail of the snake. This allows the heat to burn away from the flat and towards the point. You can also move the brisket around during the cooking, but I like keeping the smoker closed for a longer period of time.

Room Temperature Brisket?
Absolutely not. Put your brisket cold on the smoker. Why? Cold meat takes longer to start cooking. Therefore, your slab of meat sits in the smoker and takes on more smoke at the beginning of the cook. No. It doesn't lengthen your cook time, at least, not in a way that has caused me problems.

Temperature
Cook temp on my kettle using the snake can range between 225-250°F, 275°F ain't bad, either. As far as the meat, the only time I think about the temperature is when I start probing for tenderness when the center hits 197°.

Foil boat
After about 4-6 hours, I place the brisket in a foil boat. I wait for the fat to get some of that beautiful smoke color.

Rest
Once I get the correct tenderness, I move to rest. Wrapping in foil or butcher paper here is ok. I prefer to set it in a cooler for 2-3 hours. An hour MINIMUM.

Slicing
You've toiled to cook your ideal brisket. Don't ruin it at this step. Slice across the grain. Always

All the best. KEEP THE SMOKE CLEAN.

WRANGLING FIRE Achunchigan Lattore

ACKNOWLEDGEMENTS

Writing a book is a journey that requires the support and encouragement of many. I am deeply grateful to those who have helped me make **Wrangling Fire** a reality.

First and foremost, I want to thank my wife, Susie, for her unwavering belief in me and my dreams. Her support has been the foundation upon which **Cookin Wid Kunchi** and **Wrangling Fire** is built.

I am indebted to Chad and La-Shanna for capturing the essence of my work through stunning photography. Jimmy's invaluable contributions to both my written and video content have been instrumental to my success. Bryan's tireless efforts in supporting me at events have been essential to building my audience. B&B Charcoal for their unwavering support in this process has been a huge boost.

And to my incredible audience, thank you for your passion and enthusiasm. Your support has pushed me to new heights and inspired me to create this book.

I am eternally grateful for each and every one of you.

WRANGLING FIRE Achunchigan Lattore

THANK YOU FOR READING!

with smoke

www.cookinwidkunchi.com

YOUR NOTES:

YOUR NOTES:

Made in the USA
Las Vegas, NV
06 October 2024

817478ce-c86d-4bfa-adb0-86c7d1428f2eR07